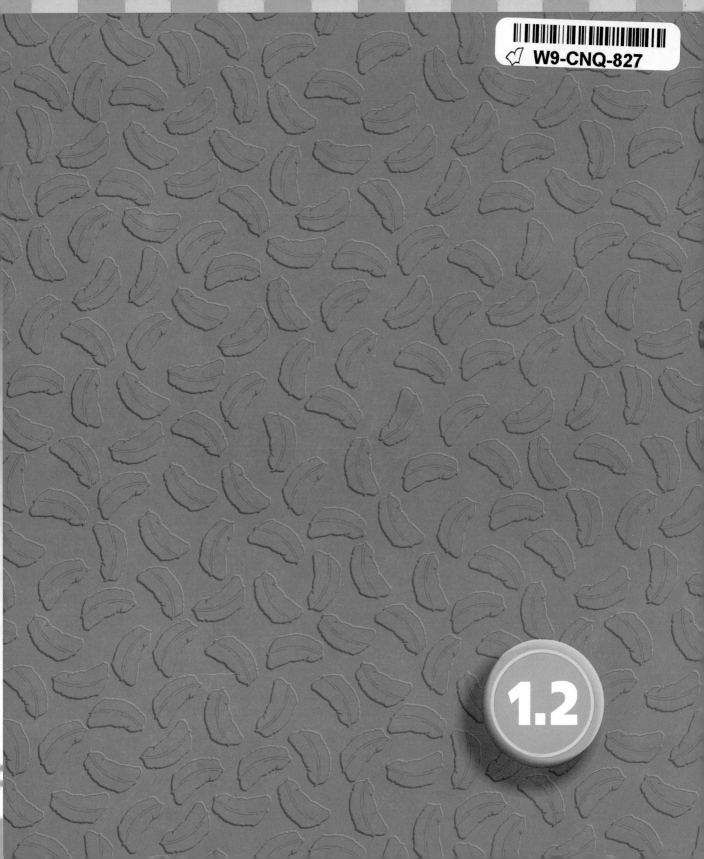

1.2

Hello, Reader!

Do you like to play with
your friends? Do you like to
look for creatures in the sea
or teach your pet special
tricks? In this book, you will
read about characters that
do these things. You may even
help solve a mystery or two!

Get ready to read
Let's Be Friends.

HOUGHTON MIFFLIN

Reading

★ Georgia ★

Let's Be Friends

Senior Authors
J. David Cooper
John J. Pikulski

Authors
Patricia A. Ackerman
Kathryn H. Au
David J. Chard
Gilbert G. Garcia
Claude N. Goldenberg
Marjorie Y. Lipson
Susan E. Page
Shane Templeton
Sheila W. Valencia
MaryEllen Vogt

Consultants
Linda H. Butler
Linnea C. Ehri
Carla B. Ford

 HOUGHTON MIFFLIN   BOSTON • MORRIS PLAINS, NJ

California • Colorado • Georgia • Illinois • New Jersey • Texas

Cover and title page photography by Tony Scarpetta.

Cover illustration by Anna Rich.

Acknowledgments begin on page 163.

Printed in the U.S.A.

ISBN: 0-618-25085-9

3 4 5 6 7 8 9 DW 11 10 09 08 07 06 05

Let's Look Around! 12

Big Book: Pearl's First Prize Plant
by A. Delaney

fiction

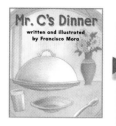

fantasy

Phonics Library:
Lots of Picking
Bill Bird
Tim's Cat

4

Big Book: Hilda Hen's Scary Night
by Mary Wormell

🏅 Bank Street College Best Children's
Books of the Year

fantasy

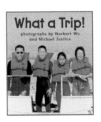

nonfiction

Phonics Library:
Let's Trim the Track!
Brad's Quick Rag Tricks
Fran Pig's Brick Hut

Additional Resources

On My Way
Practice Readers

Mack
by James M. Pare

Apple Picking
by Irma Singer

The Crab
by Alice E. Lisson

Theme Paperbacks

Barnyard Tracks
by Dee Dee Duffy
illustrated by Janet Marshall

Mud!
by Charnan Simon
photographs by
Dorothy Handelman

When Tiny Was Tiny
by Cari Meister
illustrated by Rich Davis

Family and Friends   84

Phonics Library:
Hot Dog
Tom's Plan
Jock's Hut

realistic
fiction

Big Book: The Secret Code
by Dana Meachen Rau
illustrated by Bari Weissman

realistic
fiction

Phonics Library:
Knock, Knock
Miss Nell
Deb and Bess

Big Book: Caribbean Dream
by Rachel Isadora
🎗 Americas Award Commended List

realistic
fiction

realistic
fiction

Phonics Library:
Buzzing Bug
Duff in the Mud
Jess and Mom

9

On My Way Practice Readers

Family Day
by Naomi Parker

Best Friends
by Ann Takman

The Bug Jug Band
by Dan McDaniel

Theme Paperbacks

Biscuit Finds a Friend
by Alyssa Satin Capucilli
illustrated by Pat Schories

Come! Sit! Speak!
by Charnan Simon
illustrated by Bari Weissman

The Day the Sheep Showed Up
by David McPhail

To read about more good books, go to
Education Place.

www.eduplace.com/kids

· ·

This Internet reading incentive program provides
thousands of titles for children to read.

www.bookadventure.org

Let's Look Around!

Teacher Read Aloud

Sleeping Outdoors

Under the dark
is a star,

Under the star
is a tree,

Under the tree
is a blanket,

And under the
blanket is me.

by Marchette Chute

13

Seasons

written by Michael Medearis

Words to Know

animal	see
bird	cap
cold	fat
fall	nap
flower	pack
full	bugs
look	lots
of	sacks

It is fall.

Jack can get a cap.

It can get cold.

14

Jack can get a flower.
Jack can see a bird. Tap, tap, tap!
It can get lots of big, fat bugs.

Look! The fat animal can nap.
Dad and Jack pack sacks full
of nuts.

Meet the Author
Michael Medearis

Seasons

written by Michael Medearis

It Is Fall

It can get cool.
We can jump in the leaves!

Rick can pack ten big sacks
full of leaves.

Birds can go south.
Animals can get fat, fat, fat.

It Is Winter

It can get cold.
Does it get cold where you live?

An animal can get set to nap.
It can dig a big den.

Wet snow can fall.
You can have fun in snow!

Look at the big snowman!
Dad can help.

Bill has a cap for his snowman.

It Is Spring

It can get wet.
Will Jill get wet? Not yet!

Tap, tap, tap!
A bird can peck and get bugs.
Jack will tap and get sap.

Jenn has a spring flower.
Jenn will see lots of spring flowers.

It Is Summer

It can get hot.
It is fun to get wet in the hot sun.

Nick can sit and get wet.
Nick is not hot!

Ross has a fan.
Ross is not hot!

Matt has a big net and his red box.

Quick, Matt! Get the net!
Jeff and his dad got a big bass!

Think About the Story

Seasons

written by Michael Medearis

1 How do animals get ready for the different seasons?

2 What different things do people do in different seasons? Why?

3 What happens during the seasons where you live?

34

Write a Sentence

Write a sentence about your favorite season.

I can swim in the summer!

35

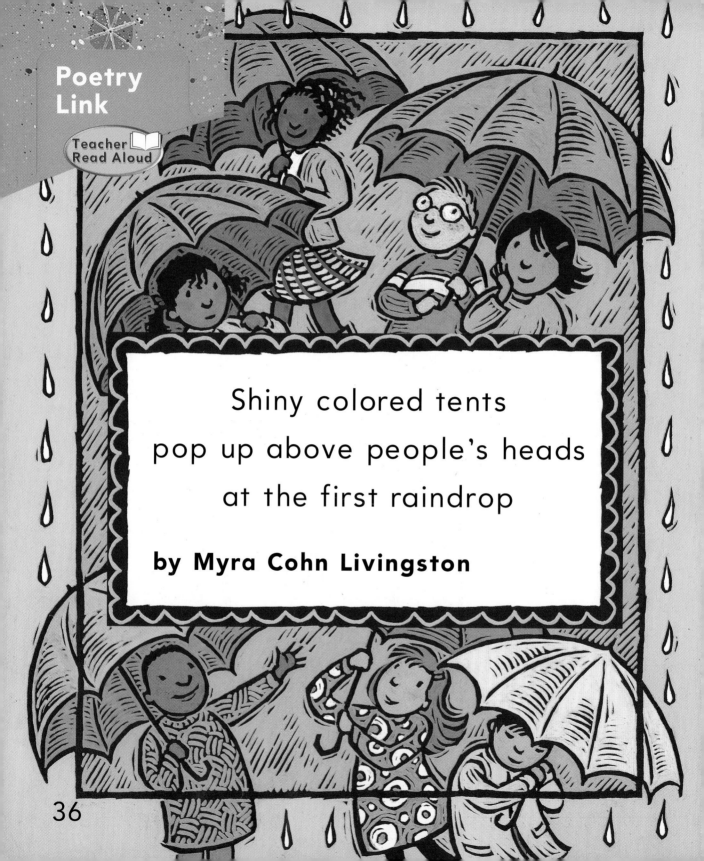

Shiny colored tents

pop up above people's heads

at the first raindrop

by Myra Cohn Livingston

Here we are, Winter,
just you and I in the snow,
freezing together

by Myra Cohn Livingston

Mr. C's Dinner

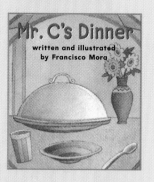

Mr. C's Dinner
written and illustrated
by Francisco Mora

Words to Know

all	first	bib
call	never	in
why	will	lips
paper	miss	asked
eat	Pig	jumped
every	big	backing
shall	six	licking

A big ad in Fox's paper said, "Eat all you can at Big C's." Fox jumped up. "Big C's is fun! I will call and ask Pig."

"Pig, will you eat at Big C's?" asked Fox.
"Why not?" said Pig. "I never miss it!
Shall we go at six, Fox?"

Pig had every bib in a big bag.
"Who will go in first?" asked Pig,
licking his big lips.
"Not I, Pig," said Fox, backing up.

Meet the Author and Illustrator
Francisco Mora

Mr. C's Dinner

written and illustrated
by Francisco Mora

Dot Hen got a paper.

Sid Fox got a paper in his box.

Lil Pig got a paper, too.
It had a map on it.

"I shall not miss it at six,"
said Lil Pig.

"We shall go, but who is Mr. C?"
they asked.
"Is it a big, bad trick?"

They all met at Mr. C's den at six.
A big tag said, "Mr. C's Den."
"Mr. C lives here," said Dot Hen.

Lil Pig got every animal a big bib.

Sid Fox sat, licking his lips.
"Where is Mr. C?" he asked.

"Sid, call Mr. C," said Dot Hen.
Sid Fox called, "Mr. C! Mr. C!"

Tap, tap, tap. It is Mr. C!
"Look!" yelled Sid Fox.
"Mr. C is Cal Coyote! Run! Run!"

Lil Pig jumped up.
Dot Hen jumped up.
"Will you eat us?" asked Lil Pig,
backing away.

"Never!" said Mr. C.
"It is not a big, bad trick.
Who will eat first?"

"I will," said Dot Hen.
"Why not? Yams! Yum, yum!"

Think About the Story

1 Why did Mr. C send the invitation?

2 How did the animals feel when they found out who Mr. C was? Why?

3 What would you do if you got an invitation from Mr. C?

Make a List

Write a list of other foods Mr. C might serve at dinner. Make a dinner menu using your list.

What do you call two banana peels?
A pair of slippers!

Where did the hamburgers go to dance?
The meatball

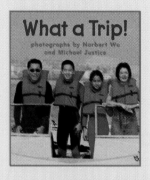

What a Trip!
photographs by Norbert Wu
and Michael Justice

Words to Know

also	some
funny	trap
green	crab
color	grab
like	crack
brown	it's
many	let's
blue	

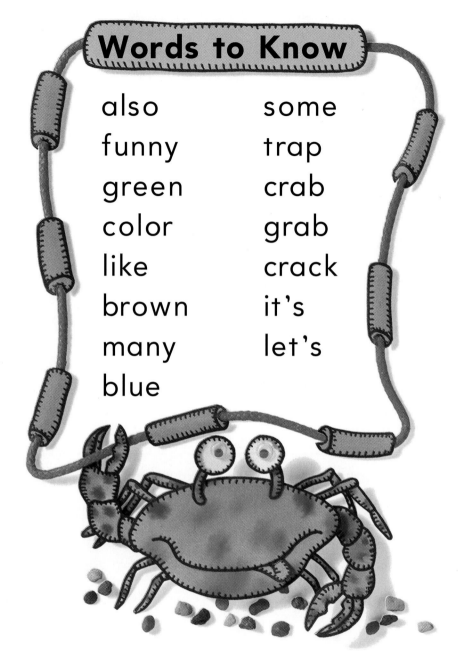

Dad has a big net. It's wet!
What is in the big wet net?
It has some big crabs in it!

Many crabs are a blue color.
Lots of crabs are brown, also.
Can Dad trap a funny green crab?
I like crabs!

A crab can run on the sand.
It can grab. Crack! Crack!
Quick, Dad! Let's trap a crab!

Meet the Photographer
Norbert Wu

What a Trip!

photographs by Norbert Wu
and Michael Justice

Let's go on a fun trip!
Let's get wet, wet, wet!

Get set! Jump in!
I jump in. Dad and Greg jump in.
What will we see?

65

Here is a funny big fish!
It has big fins. It also has big lips!

Here is a big, fat blue fish!
What is it looking at?

It's a big brown crab!
A crab can run on the sand.
It has many legs.
Quick! Quick! Let's trap it!

A crab can grab.
What can it grab?
What can it crack?
Crack, crack, crack!

Here is a big green fish.
It also has blue on it.

It's a big, big whale!
It can eat a lot.
Many whales like krill.

krill

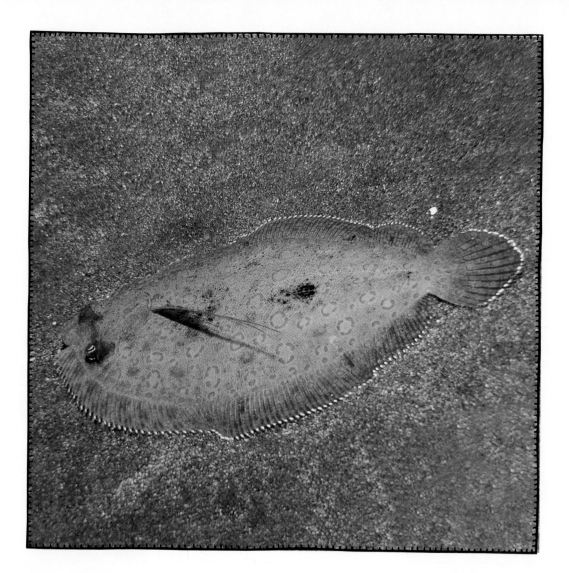

Some fish can change color.

What a trick!

Look! It is on the sand.

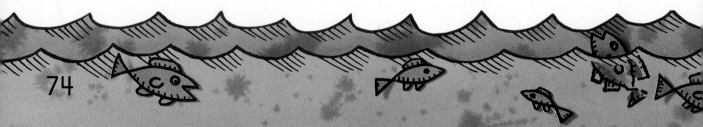

Some fish can prick.
Do not grab it!
It's not fun to get pricked.

Fish can zig zag in the rocks.
Zig zag, zig zag!
Is it fun?

Quick! Let's zig zag back.
Mom can help us get back in.

Dad grins at us.
We drip and drip, but we had fun.
What a trip!

Think About the Story

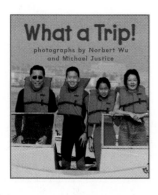

1 How are the fish in the story different?

2 Which fish would you like to learn more about? Why?

3 Would you like to go on a trip like this? Why?

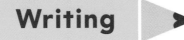

Write a Sentence

Write a sentence about your favorite part of the story.

I liked the whale eating krill.

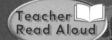
One, two, three, four, five

One, two, three, four, five,
Once I caught a fish alive.
Six, seven, eight, nine, ten,
Then I let it go again.

Why did you let it go?
Because it bit my finger so.
Which finger did it bite?
This little finger on my right.

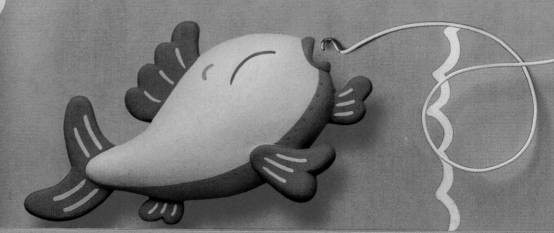

82

Family and Friends

Little pictures
Hang above me.
Pictures of the folks
Who love me.
Mom and Dad
And Uncle Jack,
They love me...
I love them back.

by Arnold Lobel

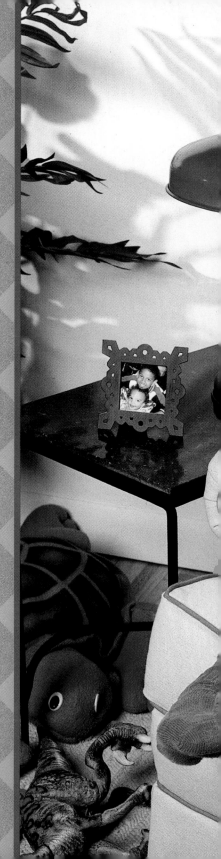

Who's in a Family?

Words to Know

children	picture
come	your
family	dog
father	on
love	lots
mother	plan
people	click

Come look at a picture. It has the people in a family in it.

It has a mother and a father in it.
It has children and six pets in it.
It has a black dog on a lap.
It has Mom, Dad, Tom, and me in it!

We get lots and lots of love.
Plan to get your family in a big picture.
Who will get in it?
Click, click, click!

Meet the Author
Sheila Kelly

Meet the Author
and Photographer
Shelley Rotner

Who's in a Family?

written by
Sheila Kelly
and Shelley Rotner

photographs by
Shelley Rotner

Who is in a family?
Quick! Come on! Get set!
Let's see some family pictures.

A mom can snap a picture.
Click, click, click!
Mom is glad to have a picture!

Click, click, click!
Children are in families.

Click, click, click!
A family can have a mother
and a father.

Click, click, click!
Moms can get big hugs.
Dads can get big hugs.
People can get lots and lots of love.

Click, click, click!
Some pets are in pictures.

Click, click!
Fluff is a pet cat.

Click, click!
Cliff is a big, pet dog.

Click, click, click!
A family can dig and plant a
big garden.

Click, click, click!
A family can jog. Run, run, run!
They jog on a flat track.
They can jog six quick laps!

Click, click, click!
A family can grill hot food
at a picnic. Yum! Yum!

Click, click, click!
A family can play. Toss the red ball.
Quick, grab it! Toss it back!
It did not drop!

Quick! Get set!
Plan to get your family picture.

Click, click, click!
Get in the picture!

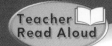
Think About the Story

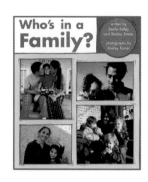
Who's in a Family?
written by
Sheila Kelly
and Shelley Rotner
photographs by
Shelley Rotner

1 How are the families the same?

2 How are they different?

3 Does your family do any of the things in the story? What are they?

Write a List

Write a list of some things that families like to do together.

Things Families Like
to Do Together

fish

paint

cook

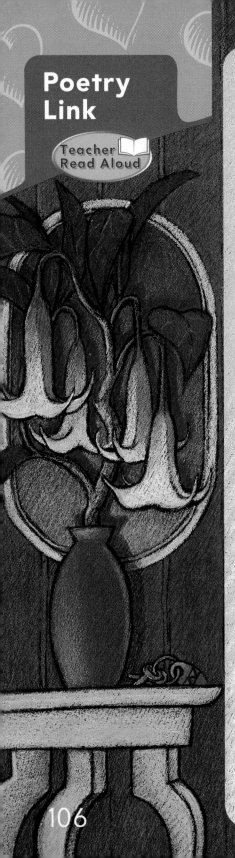

Good Night

Goodnight Mommy
Goodnight Dad

I kiss them as I go

Goodnight Teddy
Goodnight Spot

The moonbeams call me so

I climb the stairs
Go down the hall
And walk into my room

My day of play is ending
But my night of sleep's
 in bloom

by Nikki Giovanni

107

The Best Pet
written and illustrated
by Anna Rich

Words to Know

friend	best
girl	Peg
know	pet
play	swell
read	ten
she	bells
sing	knock
today	Slim
write	wrist

My best friend is a girl called Peg. She has a pet called Slim Jim. Slim Jim is a fun pet.

Can Slim Jim get in a pet test?
Read what I write to Peg today.

Does Slim Jim know
a swell trick?

Peg writes back and
tells me Slim Jim's tricks.

Slim Jim can play a swell
trick. He can sit on my
wrist. Slim Jim can sing
and knock on ten bells.

Slim Jim is Peg's best pet!

Meet the Author and Illustrator
Anna Rich

The Best Pet

**written and illustrated
by Anna Rich**

Jen's best friend is Peg.
Peg's pet is Slim.

Slim can sing and skip.
Slim can play on big blocks.
She is a fun pet!

One day Jen looked at a big sign.

"Read it, Peg!" gasped Jen.

"Peg, write in and get Slim in the
Best Pet Test," said Jen.

"What can Slim do well?"
Peg asked.

"I know!" said Jen. "I will
tell you a swell plan!"

Today is the Best Pet Test!
Lots of pets are here.

A girl has pet frogs. The frogs
do jumping and kicking tricks
in a box.

Next is Smog, a big black
and tan dog. Smog has a trick
on ten bells.

Lots of pets did tricks,
but Slim did the best pet trick!

Slim sat still on Peg's wrist.
Peg said, "Knock! Knock!"

Slim asked, "Who's there?"

"Ben," said Peg.
"Ben who?" asked Slim.

"Ben knocking on your door all day," said Peg.

Everyone yelled, "Slim! Slim!
Slim's pet trick is best!"

Jen and Peg felt glad.
Slim fluffed and puffed.
She felt glad, too.
Slim got first prize!

Think About the Story

The Best Pet
written and illustrated
by Anna Rich

1 Why do you think the girls entered Slim in the Best Pet Test?

2 Do you think Slim did the best trick? Why?

3 What trick would you teach Slim for the Best Pet Test?

128

Write a Description

Write a sentence about your favorite character or pet from the story.

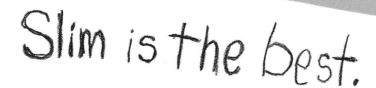

129

Knock-knock.
Who's there?
Cows go.
Cows go who?
Cows don't go who,
they go moo.

Knock-knock.
Who's there?
You.
You who?
Are you calling me?

131

Bud's Day Out

Bud's Day Out
written by G. Brian Karas
illustrated by Clive Scruton

Words to Know

car	their	hug
down	walk	Bud
hear	would	fuss
hold	run	must
hurt	fun	scrub
learn	but	splat

Mom and Dad get in their
big car. I can not hold Bud.
"Walk," I tell Bud. "Do not run."

Bud can not hear me.
Bud runs down to the car.
Splat! Bud is not hurt,
but I must scrub up.
I fuss and fuss. It is not fun!

"Bud, would a big, big hug
help you learn?" I ask.

Meet the Author
G. Brian Karas

Meet the Illustrator
Clive Scruton

Bud's Day Out

written by G. Brian Karas

illustrated by Clive Scruton

Bud is Ben's big black dog. Every day
Ben would run in and hug Bud.

Bud would run up and down,
but not today.

"Where is Bud, Mom? Is Bud
in back?" asked Ben.
"Let's look for him," said Mom.

Ben felt sad and asked,
"Is Bud hurt?"
"Bud is not hurt," said Mom.

Ben ran and got in their car.
"Hold on," said Mom. "Let's walk."

Ben and Mom walked and met Dan.
Ben asked, "Did a big black dog
run in?"

"Not today," said Dan.
"Why not stop in the glass shop
and ask Miss Jill?"

Ben and Mom walked in.
"Miss Jill, did a big black dog run in?"
asked Ben.

"Not today," said Miss Jill.
"Why not stop in the pet shop?"

"Mom, did you just hear a dog?"
Ben asked. "Quick! Run! I know
where Bud is!"

"Yip, yip! Yap, yap!" yelped Bud.
Bud ran up and down.
Animals ran up and down.
Splat! Splat! Splat!

What a big mess!
"Stop! Stop! Stop!" yelled Mr. Plum.
"Grab the dog!"

"Come, Bud!" yelled Ben.
Ben got Bud. Bud got a big hug.

Mom gasped, "Let's help
scrub up the big mess."
Mr. Plum felt glad.

"Bud must learn *The Ten Rules for Dogs*," said Mr. Plum.
Ben yelled, "What fun! I can read, and Bud can look at the pictures!"

Teacher
Read Aloud

Think About the Story

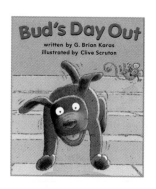

Bud's Day Out
written by G. Brian Karas
illustrated by Clive Scruton

1 How did Ben know where to find Bud?

2 Why did Bud need to learn rules?

3 What would you say to Bud?

Write a Sentence

Write a rule for Bud.

Do not run in the shop.

Where, Oh Where Has My Little Dog Gone?

Oh where, oh where has
my little dog gone?
Oh where, oh where can he be?
With his ears cut short
and his tail cut long,
Oh where, oh where is he?

Word Lists

Seasons

Target Skills:

double final consonants
bass, Bill, Jeff, Jenn, Jill, Matt, Ross, will

blending more short *a* words
bass, has, Jack, Matt, pack, sacks

final consonants (*s* as /z/, *ck*)
bugs, has, his, Jack, Nick, pack, peck, quick, Rick, sacks

plurals with *s*
bugs, lots, sacks

Words Using Previously Taught Skills:
an, at, big, box, can, cap, Dad, den, dig, fan, fat, fun, get, got, help, hot, it, nap, net, red, sap, set, sit, sun, tap, ten, wet, yet

SKILLS APPLIED IN WORDS IN STORY: consonants *m, s, c, t;* short *a;* consonants *n, f, p;* consonants *b, r, h, g;* short *i;* consonants *d, w, l, x;* short *o,* consonants *k, y;* short *e;* consonants *j, q;* short *u*

New
animal/animals, bird/birds, cold, fall, flower/flowers, full, look, of, see

Previously Taught
a, and, does, for, go, have, in, is, jump, live, not, the, to, we, where, you

cool, leaves, seasons, snow, snowman, south, spring, summer, winter

Mr. C's Dinner

Target Skills:

verb endings -s, -ed, -ing
asked, backing, licking, yelled

possessives ('s)
C's, Fox's, Hen's, Pig's

blending more short *i* words
licking, lips, miss, six, will

Words Using Previously Taught Skills:

at, bad, bib, big, box, but, C, Cal, den, Dot, Fox, get, got, had, Hen, his, it, Lil, map, met, Mr., Pig, run, sat, Sid, tag, tap, up, us, yams, yum

SKILLS APPLIED IN WORDS IN STORY: consonants *m, s, c, t;* short *a;* consonants *n, f, p;* consonants *b, r, h, g;* short *i;* consonants *d, w, l, x;* short *o,* consonants *k, y;* short *e;* short *u;* double final consonants; final consonants (*s* as /z/, *ck*); blending more short *a* words; plurals with -*s*

New
all, call/called, eat, every, first, never, paper, shall, why

Previously Taught
a, animal, away, go, he, here, I, in, is, jumped, lives, look, my, not, on, said, they, too, we, where, who, you

Coyote, dinner, trick

What a Trip!

Target Skills:

consonant clusters with *r*

crab, crack, drip, grab, Greg, grins, krill, prick, pricked, trap, trick, trip

contractions with -'s

it's, let's

Words Using Previously Taught Skills:

at, back, big, but, can, Dad, fat, fins, fun, get, had, has, help, it, legs, lips, lot, Mom, quick, rocks, run, sand, set, up, us, wet, will, zag, zig

SKILLS APPLIED IN WORDS IN STORY: consonants *m, s, c, t;* short *a;* consonants *n, f, p;* consonants *b, r, h, g;* short *i;* consonants *d, w, l;* short *o;* consonant *k;* short *e;* consonants *q, z;* short *u;* double final consonants; final consonants (*s* as /z/, *ck*); plurals with *-s;* verb ending *-ed;* blending more short *i* words

HIGH-FREQUENCY WORDS

New

also, blue, brown, color, funny, green, like, many, some

Previously Taught

a, and, do, eat, go, here, I, in, is, jump, look/looking, not, on, see, the, to, we, what

STORY WORDS

change, fish, whales

159

Who's in a Family?

Target Skills:

consonant clusters with *l*
click, Cliff, flat, Fluff, glad, plan, plant

blending more short *o* words
drop, jog, lots, moms, toss

Words Using Previously Taught Skills:
at, back, big, can, cat, dads, did, dig, dog, get, grab, grill, hot, hugs, it, laps, let's, mom, pet, pets, quick, run, set, six, track, yum

SKILLS APPLIED IN WORDS IN STORY: consonants *m, s, c, t;* short *a;* consonants *n, f, p;* consonants *b, r, h, g;* short *i;* consonants *d, l, x;* short *o;* consonants *k, y;* short *e;* consonants *q, j;* short *u;* double final consonants; final consonants *(s* as /z/, *ck);* plurals with *-s;* consonant clusters with *r;* contractions with *-'s*

HIGH-FREQUENCY WORDS

New
children, come, family, father, love, mother, people, picture/pictures, your

Previously Taught
a, and, are, have, in, is, not, of, on, play, some, the, they, to, who, who's

STORY WORDS
ball, families, food, garden, picnic, snap

The Best Pet

DECODABLE WORDS

Target Skills:

consonant clusters with *s*
asked, best, gasped, skip, Slim, Slim's, Smog, still, swell, test, wrist

blending more short *e* words
bells, best, felt, next, swell, tell, test, well, yelled

silent consonants *kn, wr, gn*
knock, knocking, sign, wrist

Words Using Previously Taught Skills:
at, Ben, big, black, blocks, box, but, can, did, dog, fluffed, frogs, fun, get, glad, got, has, it, Jen, Jen's, kicking, lots, Peg, Peg's, pet, pets, plan, puffed, sat, tan, ten, trick, tricks, will

SKILLS APPLIED IN WORDS IN STORY: consonants *m, s, c, t;* short *a;* consonants *n, f, p;* consonants *b, r, h, g;* short *i;* consonants *d, w, l, x;* short *o;* consonants *k, y;* short *e;* consonant *j;* short *u;* double final consonants; final consonants *(s* as /z/, *ck);* plurals with *-s;* verb endings *-ed, -ing;* possessives *('s);* consonant clusters with *r;* consonant clusters with *l;* blending more short *o* words

The Best Pet continued

New

friend, girl, know, play, read, she, sing, today, write

Previously Taught

a, all, and, are, come, do, first, here, I, in, is, jumping, looked, of, on, one, said, the, too, what, who, who's, you, your

day, door, everyone, prize, sign, there

Bud's Day Out

Target Skills:

triple clusters

scrub, splat

blending more short *u* words

just, must, Plum, scrub

Words Using Previously Taught Skills:

ask, asked, at, back, Ben, big, black, Bud, Bud's, but, can, Dan, did, dog, dogs, felt, fun, gasped, glad, glass, got, grab, help, him, his, hug, Jill, let's, mess, Miss, Mom, Mr., pet, quick, ran, run, sad, stop, ten, up, yap, yelled, yelp, yelped, yip

SKILLS APPLIED IN WORDS IN STORY: consonants *m, s, c, t;* short *a;* consonants *n, f, p;* consonants *b, r, h, g;* short *i;* consonants *d, l;* short *o;* consonants *k, y;* short *e;* consonants *q, j;* short *u;* double final consonants; final consonants (*s* as /z/, *ck*); plurals with *-s;* verb ending *-ed;* possessives (*'s*); contractions with *-'s;* consonant clusters with *l;* blending more short *o* words; consonant clusters with *s;* blending more short *e* words

New

car, down, hear, hold, hurt, learn, their, walk/walked, would

Previously Taught

a, and, animals, come, every, for, I, in, is, know, look, not, on, pictures, read, said, the, today, what, where, why, you

day, out, rules, shop

HIGH-FREQUENCY WORDS TAUGHT TO DATE

a	friend	never	we
all	for	not	what
also	four	of	where
and	full	on	who
animal	funny	once	why
are	girl	one	would
away	go	paper	write
bird	green	people	you
blue	have	picture	your
brown	he	play	
call	hear	pull	
car	here	read	
children	hold	said	
cold	hurt	see	
color	I	shall	
come	in	she	
do	is	sing	
does	jump	some	
down	know	the	
eat	learn	their	
every	like	they	
fall	live	three	
family	look	to	
father	love	today	
find	many	too	
first	me	two	
five	mother	upon	
flower	my	walk	

Decoding skills taught to date: consonants *m, s, c, t;* short *a;* consonants *n, f, p;* consonants *b, r, h, g;* short *i;* consonants *d, w, l, x;* short *o;* consonants *k, v, y;* short *e;* consonants *q, j, z;* short *u;* double final consonants; final consonants (*s* as /z/, *ck*); plurals with -*s;* blending more short *a* words; verb endings -*s, -ed, -ing;* possesives ('*s*); blending more short *i* words; consonant clusters with *r;* contractions with -'*s;* consonant clusters with *l;* blending more short *o* words; consonant clusters with *s;* blending more short *e* words; silent consonants *kn, wr, gn;* triple clusters; blending more short *u* words.

Acknowledgments

For each of the selections listed below, grateful acknowledgment is made for permission to excerpt and/or reprint original or copyrighted material, as follows:

Poetry

"Good Night" from *Vacation Time, Poems for Children,* by Nikki Giovanni. Copyright © 1980 by Nikki Giovanni. Reprinted by permission of HarperCollins Publishers.

"Here we are, Winter" from *Cricket Never Does,* by Myra Cohn Livingston, illustrated by Kees de Kiefte. Text copyright © 1997 by Myra Cohn Livingston. Reprinted by permission of Margaret K. McElderry Books, an imprint of Simon & Schuster Children's Publishing Division.

Selection from *Kids Are Punny 2: More Jokes Sent by Kids to "The Rosie O'Donnell Show."* Copyright © 1998 by The For All Kids Foundation. Reprinted by permission of The For All Kids Foundation.

"Little Pictures" from *Whiskers & Rhymes,* by Arnold Lobel. Copyright © 1985 by Arnold Lobel. Reprinted by permission of HarperCollins Publishers.

"Shiny Colored Tents" from *Cricket Never Does,* by Myra Cohn Livingston, illustrated by Kees de Kiefte. Text copyright © 1997 by Myra Cohn Livingston. Reprinted by permission of Margaret K. McElderry Books, an imprint of Simon & Schuster Children's Publishing Division.

"Sleeping Outdoors" from *Rhymes About Us,* by Marchette Chute, published in 1974 by E.P. Dutton. Copyright © by Marchette Chute. Reprinted by permission of Elizabeth Hauser.

Credits

Photography

3 (t) Ross Hamilton/Tony Stone Images. **7** (t) image Copyright © 2000 PhotoDisc, Inc. **12** (icon) Ross Hamilton/Tony Stone Images. **16** Andrew Yates/Mercury Pictures. **17** Richard Price/FPG International. **18** Donna Day/Tony Stone Images. **19** Mitch York/Tony Stone Images. **20** (t) Tim Davis/Tony Stone Images. (b) Daniel Cox/Tony Stone Images. **21** R.G.K. Photography/Tony Stone Images. **22** John Warden/Tony Stone Images. **23** Rob Casey/Tony Stone Images. **24** Lori Adamski Peek/Tony Stone Images. **25** Rommel/MASTERFILE. **26** Rommel/MASTERFILE. **27** (l) Jack Wilburn/Animals Animals. (r) Ted Levine/Animals Animals/Earth Scenes. **28** Chad Ehlers/Tony Stone Images. **29** Michael Agliolo/International Stock. **30** Gene Peach Photography/Liaison Agency. **32** Corbis Royalty Free. **33** Mug Shots/The Stock Market. **40** Courtesy Francisco Mora. **62** Norbert Wu Productions. **66-80** Norbert Wu Productions. **70** (shell) image Copyright © 2000 PhotoDisc, Inc. **84** (icon) image Copyright © 2000 PhotoDisc, Inc. **88** (t) © Shelly Rotner. (b) © Emily Calcagnino. **89–104** © Shelly Rotner. **110** Mike Tamborrino/Mercury Pictures. **128** image Copyright © 2000 PhotoDisc, Inc. **134** (t) Jon Crispin/Mercury Pictures. (b) Steve Benbow/Mercury Pictures. **152** image Copyright © 2000 PhotoDisc, Inc..

Assignment Photography

13, 34–5, 56–7, 81, 84–5, 105, 129, 153 David Bradley Photographer. **31, 63–5, 78–9** Michael Justice/Mercury Pictures.

Illustration

12–13 Chris Butler. **14–35** (bkgs) Linda Helton. **36–37** Bonnie MacKain. **38–55** Francisco X. Mora. **58–59** Vince Andriani. **60–79** Franklin Hammond. **82–83** Tomohiro Kikuchi. **86–87** Ruth Flanigan. **106–107** Siri Weber Feeney. **108–127** Anna Rich. **130–131** Tim Haggerty. **132–151** Clive Scruton. **154–155** Martha Aviles.